Oxford First
Maths
Dictionary

Compiled by Peter Patilla

Illustrated by Georgie Birkett

OXFORD
UNIVERSITY PRESS

My name is

OXFORD
UNIVERSITY PRESS

Great Clarendon Street, Oxford OX2 6DP

Oxford University Press is a department of the University of Oxford.
It furthers the University's objective of excellence in research, scholarship,
and education by publishing worldwide in

Oxford New York

Auckland Bangkok Buenos Aires Cape Town Chennai
Dar es Salaam Delhi Hong Kong Istanbul Karachi Kolkata
Kuala Lumpur Madrid Melbourne Mexico City Mumbai Nairobi
São Paulo Shanghai Taipei Tokyo Toronto

Oxford is a registered trade mark of Oxford University Press
in the UK and in certain other countries

Text copyright © Peter Patilla 2001
Illustrations by Georgie Birkett

The moral rights of the author/artist have been asserted

Database right Oxford University Press (maker)

First published 2001
This edition published 2004

British Library Cataloguing in Publication Data available

Hardback ISBN 0–19–911163-4
Paperback ISBN 0–19–911164-2
Big book ISBN 0-19-911167-7

1 3 5 7 9 10 8 6 4 2

Printed in Singapore

Contents

Introduction

Oxford First Maths Dictionary contains over 200 mathematical words in alphabetical order, each with a simple meaning. Colourful pictures and diagrams help to make the meanings clear.

Extra words that children will discover in their maths lessons are given at the end of the dictionary. All the words in the dictionary have been carefully chosen to support and develop mathematical language and understanding.

The main features on the A to Z pages are:

position of letter in the alphabet

alphabet

capital letter

letter

beginning letter

word

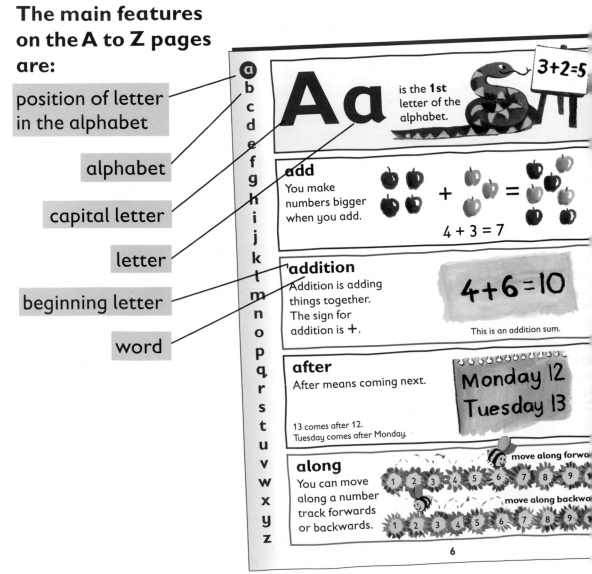

a b c d e f g h i j k l m n o p q r s t u v w x y z

Aa

is the **1st** letter of the alphabet.

3+2=5

add

You make numbers bigger when you add.

4 + 3 = 7

addition

Addition is adding things together. The sign for addition is +.

4+6=10

This is an addition sum.

after

After means coming next.

Monday 12
Tuesday 13

13 comes after 12.
Tuesday comes after Monday.

along

You can move along a number track forwards or backwards.

move along forwa
1 2 3 4 5 6 7 8 9

move along backwa
1 2 3 4 5 6 7 8 9

6

This is also an ideal introduction to reference books. It helps children learn about order and to find out how to locate a word using its first letter. They learn how to interpret information from words, pictures, and diagrams, and see mathematical symbols used in context. The dictionary has been written and illustrated to foster children's natural curiosity about numbers, shapes, and measuring.

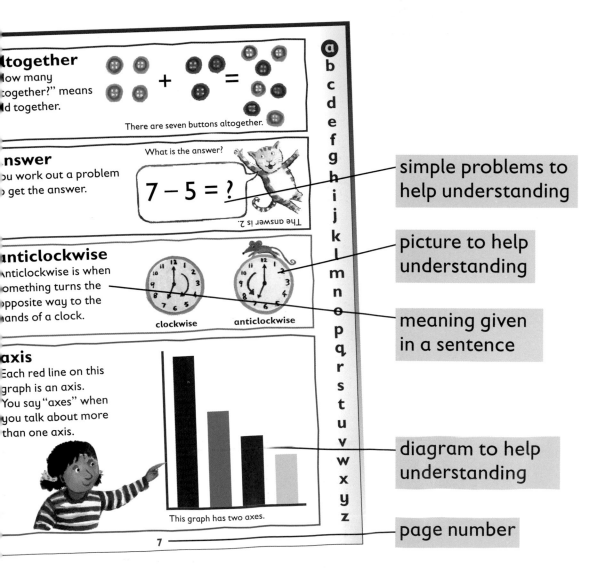

altogether
"How many together?" means add together.

There are seven buttons altogether.

answer
you work out a problem to get the answer.

What is the answer?

$7 - 5 = ?$

The answer is 2.

simple problems to help understanding

anticlockwise
Anticlockwise is when something turns the opposite way to the hands of a clock.

clockwise   anticlockwise

picture to help understanding

meaning given in a sentence

axis
Each red line on this graph is an axis. You say "axes" when you talk about more than one axis.

This graph has two axes.

diagram to help understanding

page number

7

a b c d e f g h i j k l m n o p q r s t u v w x y z

Aa

is the **1st** letter of the alphabet.

add

You make numbers bigger when you add.

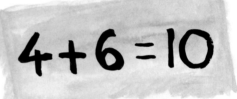

4 + 3 = 7

addition

Addition is adding things together. The sign for addition is **+**.

4 + 6 = 10

This is an addition.

after

After means coming next.

13 comes after 12.
Tuesday comes after Monday.

Monday 12
Tuesday 13

along

You can move along a number track forwards or backwards.

move along forwards

1 2 3 4 5 6 7 8 9 10

move along backwards

1 2 3 4 5 6 7 8 9 10

altogether

"How many altogether?" means add together.

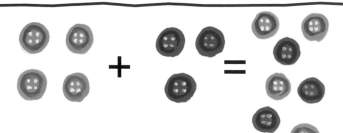

There are seven buttons altogether.

answer

You work out a problem to get the answer.

What is the answer?

$$7 - 5 = ?$$

The answer is 2.

anticlockwise

Anticlockwise is when something turns the opposite way to the hands of a clock.

clockwise   anticlockwise

axis

Each red line on this graph is an axis.
You say "axes" when you talk about more than one axis.

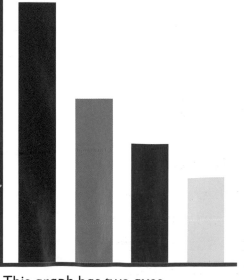

This graph has two axes.

Bb

is the **2nd** letter of the alphabet.

backwards

When you count backwards the numbers get smaller.

1 2 3 4 5 6 7 8 9 10

Count backwards from 6.

balance

Two sides balance when they are as heavy as each other.

balances

does not balance

before

Before means coming in front of.

345678

6 comes before 7.

January
February
March

January comes before February.

big

Big tells you about the size of something.

big   bigger   biggest

block graph

A block graph is made up of blocks.

This block graph tells you how many children like each colour.

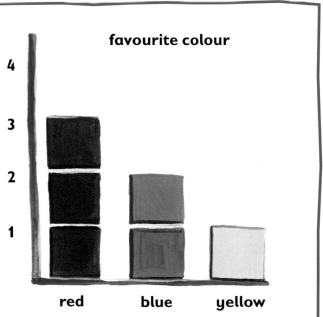

favourite colour

number of children

red   blue   yellow

button

You press the buttons on a calculator.

buy

When you buy something you pay money for it.

James buys a new ball and puts it in the bag.

C c

is the **3rd** letter of the alphabet.

calculate

When you calculate you work out the answer.

$$4 + 3$$

calendar

A calendar shows the days, weeks, and months in a year.

	March					
Mon	Tue	Wed	Thu	Fri	Sat	Sun
	1	2	3	4	5	6
7	8	9	10	11	12	13
14	15	16	17	18	19	20
21	22	23	24	25	26	27
28	29	30	31			

	April					
Mon	Tue	Wed	Thu	Fri	Sat	Sun
				1	2	3
4	5	6	7	8	9	10
11	12	13	14	15	16	17
18	19	20	21	22	23	24
25	26	27	28	29	30	

capacity

Capacity is how much something holds.

This bucket has a capacity of 8 litres.

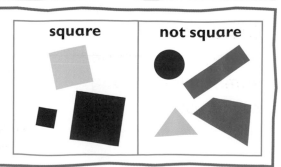

Carroll diagram

You use a Carroll diagram to sort things into groups.

square	not square

This Carroll diagram sorts shapes.

10

centimetre

A centimetre is a distance you find on some rulers. 100 centimetres is the same distance as 1 metre.

centre

The centre of a shape is exactly in the middle.

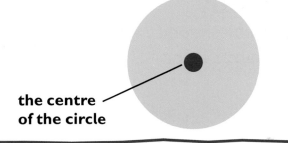

the centre of the circle

change

You get change when you pay too much money for something.

the price   you pay   your change

chart

A chart shows information.

a weather chart

cheap

Something is cheap when it does not cost a lot of money.

cheap   cheaper   cheapest

The ball is cheaper than the tractor.

circle

A circle is flat and perfectly round.

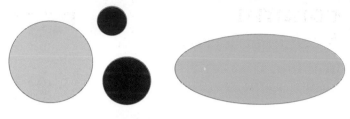

circles   **not a circle**

circular

A circular shape has a circle in it.

These shapes have circular tops.

clock

A clock shows you the time.

Some clocks have hands and numbers.   Some clocks have only numbers.

clockwise

Clockwise is when something turns the same way as the hands of a clock.

clockwise   **anticlockwise**

coin

A coin is a piece of money made from metal.

All these are coins.

column

A column of numbers goes up and down.

1	2	3	4
5	6	7	8
9	10	11	12
13	14	15	16

a column

cone

A cone has one circular end and one pointed end.

corner

The sides of a shape meet at a corner.

a corner

a corner

correct

When something is correct it is not wrong.

Which sum is correct?

$4 + 4 = 8$

$4 + 4 = 9$

4 + 4 = 8 is the correct sum.

counter

You can use counters to help you add.

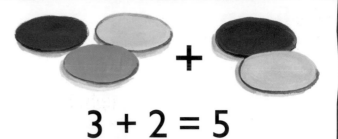

$$3 + 2 = 5$$

cube

A cube has six square faces.

All these are cubes.

cuboid

A cuboid has six rectangular faces.

All these are cuboids.

curve

A curve bends smoothly.

Here are lots of curves.

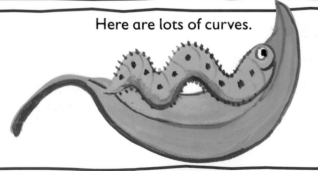

cylinder

A cylinder is a rounded shape with circular ends.

All these are cylinders.

Dd

is the **4th** letter of the alphabet.

date
The date tells you the day, the month, and the year.

Leo was born on 25th May, 1995.

dear
When something is dear it costs a lot of money.

dear **dearer** **dearest**

The red car is dearer than the yellow car.

deep
Deep is how far down or back something goes.

deep

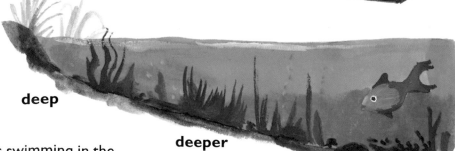

deep

deeper

deepest

The fish is swimming in the deepest end of the pond.

a b c d e f g h i j k l m n o p q r s t u v w x y z

abcdefghijklmnopqrstuvwxyz

depth

Depth is the distance from top to bottom or from front to back.

depth

diagram

A diagram shows you information in a simple way.

Here are two kinds of diagram.

Triangles

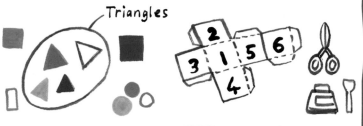

difference

To find the difference between two numbers you subtract the smaller number from the bigger one.

What is the difference between 9 and 4?

The difference is 5.

different

When something is different it is not exactly the same.

different colour

different size

digit

There are 10 digits. They are:

14

The number 14 has two digits: 1 and 4. It is a two-digit number.

0 1 2 3 4 5 6 7 8 9

digital clock

A digital clock has no hands.

a digital clock   a digital watch

distance

Distance is how far apart two things are.

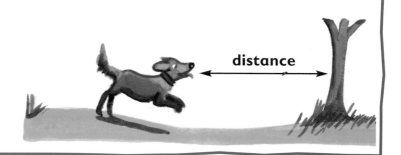

distance

divide

When you divide you share things out equally.

You can divide 6 into two equal sets of 3.

division

Division is sharing things out. The sign for division is ÷.

$6 \div 2 = 3$

This is a division.

double

When you double a number you multiply it by 2.

$5 \times 2 = 10$ Double 5 is 10.

a b c **d** e f g h i j k l m n o p q r s t u v w x y z

17

Ee

is the **5th** letter of the alphabet.

edge
The edge of a shape is where two faces meet.

curved edge

straight edge

empty
Something is empty when there is nothing inside it.

empty

equal
When two things are equal they are worth the same. The sign = tells you two things are the same.

3 + 3 are equal to 6.

$$3 + 3 = 6$$

equivalent
Equivalent things are worth the same but they look different.

Two 5p coins are equivalent to one 10p coin.

a b c d **e** f g h i j k l m n o p q r s t u v w x y z

estimate

When you estimate you make a sensible guess, not a silly one.

Estimate the number of marbles in this bag.

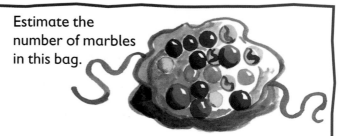

A good estimate is 20.

estimation

An estimation is a good guess.

"The ribbon is about 7 centimetres long" is a good estimation.

even

You can divide all even numbers into twos.

2 4 6 8 10 are even numbers.

exactly

Exactly means neither more nor less.

exactly the same length

nearly the same length

exchange

When you exchange something you change it for something else.

Ff

is the **6th** letter of the alphabet.

face

A face is one side of a solid shape.

curved face

flat face

fast

Fast describes how quickly something moves.

fast   faster   fastest

few

Few means a small number of things.

few   fewer   fewest

20

figure

When you write the number seventeen in figures it looks like this: **17**.

These numbers are written in figures.

flat

A flat shape is very thin.

forwards

When you count forwards the numbers get bigger.

Count forwards from 2.

fraction

A fraction is a part of a whole shape or a whole number.

a fraction of a cake

full

When something is full there is no space left inside it.

full   **half full**   **empty**

a b c d e **f** g h i j k l m n o p q r s t u v w x y z

Gg

is the **7th** letter of the alphabet.

gram

You can use grams when you weigh things.

1000 grams = 1 kilogram.

This is a 500 gram weight.

These scales weigh in grams.

graph

A graph gives you information.

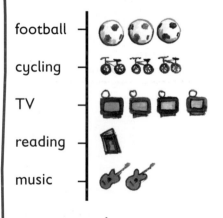

football

cycling

TV

reading

music

a pictogram

Here are two different kinds of graph.

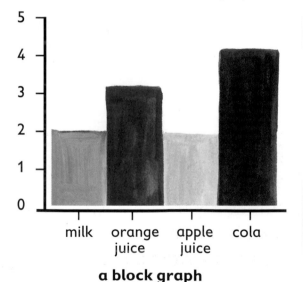

milk orange juice apple juice cola

a block graph

greater than

Greater than means more than. The sign for greater than is **>**.

5 > 2

5 is greater than 2. The > sign tells you which number is the largest.

grid

The lines on a grid go across each other.

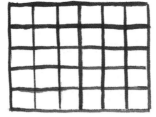

a square grid

a triangle grid

group

A group is a set of things.

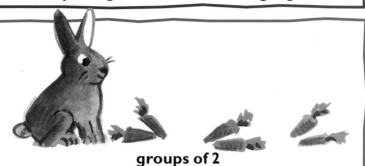

groups of 2

Hh

is the **8th** letter of the alphabet.

half

When you divide something in half each part is the same. You can write half as $\frac{1}{2}$.

half

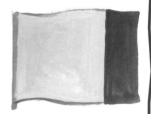

not half

half turn

A half turn is when you make half of a whole turn.

start

a half turn

a whole turn

a b c d e f **g** **h** i j k l m n o p q r s t u v w x y z

half way

Half way is in the middle.

half way

halve

When you halve something you divide it into two equal parts.

Jack halves his pear.

hand

Some clocks and watches have hands.

minute hand

hour hand

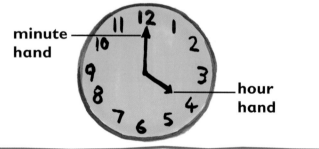

heavy

You use heavy to describe the weight of something.

heavy   heavier   heaviest

height

Height is how tall or how far something is from the ground.

height of Jenny

height of kite

hexagon

A hexagon is a flat shape with 6 straight sides.

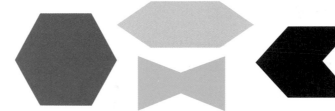

All these are hexagons.

hollow

A hollow shape is empty inside.

a hollow cube   **a hollow cylinder**

hour

One hour is 60 minutes long. There are 24 hours in each day.

One hour has passed.

hour hand

The hour hand on a clock is the shortest hand.

minute hand

hour hand

a b c d e f g h i j k l m n o p q r s t u v w x y z

I i

is the **9th** letter of the alphabet.

investigate

When you investigate you look for an answer.

Investigate the missing numbers.

irregular

The sides of an irregular shape are not the same length.

irregular shapes

J j

is the **10th** letter of the alphabet.

join

You can join up things with a line.

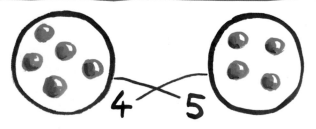

The lines join each number to a set.

Kk

is the **11th** letter of the alphabet.

kilogram

You use kilograms when you weigh heavy things. 1 kilogram = 1000 grams.

This is a **1 kilogram** weight.

Ll

is the **12th** letter of the alphabet.

label

A label tells you what something is. A title is a label.

Children's favourite ice cream

title

label

favourite ice cream

chocolate
strawberry
vanilla
mint

label

1 2 3 4
number of children

large

Large describes the size of something.

large   larger   largest

a b c d e f g h i j **k l** m n o p q r s t u v w x y z

least

The least amount is the smallest.

the least juice

left

One side of your body is the left side.

right side | left side | left side | right side

length

Length is how long something is.

length

less than

Less than means not as many as. The sign for less than is <.

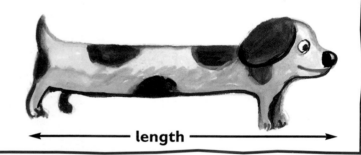

3 < 5

3 is less than 5. The < sign tells you which number is the smallest.

line

A line can be straight or curved.

a straight line

a curved line

line of symmetry

The two sides of a line of symmetry are the same.

A line of symmetry is like a mirror because one side is a reflection of the other.

a line of symmetry

list

In a list you write things under each other.

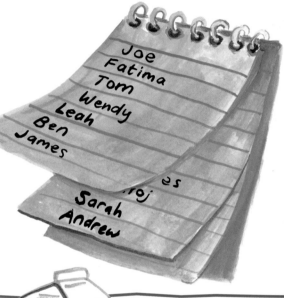

a list of names

Milk
apples
bread
cake
cheese

Joe
Fatima
Tom
Wendy
Leah
Ben
James
Sarah
Andrew

litre

You use litres when you find out how much something holds.

one litre of milk   half a litre of milk

long

Long describes the length of something.

long

longer

longest

You place things side by side to find the longest.

Mm

is the **13th** letter of the alphabet.

mass

When you weigh something you find out its mass.

The elephant has a bigger mass than the mouse.

measure

You measure something to find out its size.

measurement

A measurement is a number that tells you about the size of something.

height 114 centimetres

weight 21 kilograms

metre

You use metres to measure long lengths.

1 metre = 100 centimetres.

The side of each cube measures 1 centimetre. 100 cubes measure 1 metre.

metre stick

A metre stick is like a long ruler. It is 100 centimetres long.

a metre stick

middle

In the middle means in the centre.

6 7 8

7 is in the middle.

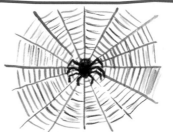

The spider is in the middle.

minus

The minus sign is —. It tells you to take away.

$7 - 4 = 3$

minute

A minute is a short time. There are 60 minutes in one hour.

Five minutes have passed.

minute hand

The minute hand moves all the way round the clock in one hour.

minute hand

a b c d e f g h i j k l m n o p q r s t u v w x y z

mirror line

A mirror line is like a mirror. One half of the picture is a reflection of the other half.

a mirror line

most

Most means the largest amount.

Alice　　**Mina**　　**Fred**

Fred has the most apples.

multiple

Here are some multiples of 2, 5, and 10.

The multiples go on and on.

multiples of 2	2, 4, 6, 8, 10 . . .
multiples of 5	5, 10, 15, 20, 25 . . .
multiples of 10	10, 20, 30, 40, 50 . . .

multiplication

Multiplication is when you multiply numbers together. The multiplication sign is **X**.

This is a multiplication.

multiply

When you multiply you add the same number again and again.

Multiply 3 by 4. What is the answer?

$3 + 3 + 3 + 3$ or $4 + 4 + 4$

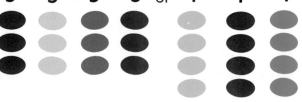

The answer is 12.

N n

is the **14th** letter of the alphabet.

narrow
When something is narrow its sides are close together.

wide

narrow

new
You use new when talking about something that is not old.

new

old

none
None is when you have nothing.

3 carrots   none

nought
Nought is another word for nothing, none, or zero.

nought, nothing, none, or zero

a b c d e f g h i j k l m **n** o p q r s t u v w x y z

number

You use numbers in many different ways.

Some ways to show the number 4.

number bond

Here are some number bonds.

addition bond	$3 + 4 = 7$
subtraction bond	$5 - 1 = 4$
multiplication bond	$2 \times 3 = 6$
division bond	$10 \div 2 = 5$

number fact

Here are some number facts for 5. You can use numbers and words.

$5 = 3 + 2$

$5 = 10 \div 2$

5 is 2 more than 3.

number line

In a number line the numbers are in order. Each number marks a point on the line.

1   2   3   4   5

Look where the numbers are in this number line.

number pair

A number pair is two numbers that go together.

5 and 5,0   4 and 4,1

3 and 2 3,2

All these number pairs total 5.

number sentence

A number sentence uses words and numbers.

6 take away 2 leaves 4

3 more than 5 makes 8

number square

In a number square a number is written inside each square.

Put your finger on number 11 and count on 6 squares. What is the answer?

1	2	3	4	5
6	7	8	9	10
11	12	13	14	15
16	17	18	19	20
21	22	23	24	25

a 25 number square

The answer is 17.

number track

In a number track the numbers are in order. Each number takes up a space on the line.

1 2 3 4 5 6 7 8 9 10

a number track

numeral

A numeral is a word or a number.

3 three III

All these are numerals.

a b c d e f g h i j k l m **n** o p q r s t u v w x y z

 **O o** is the **15th** letter of the alphabet.

oblong

An oblong is longer than it is wide.

oblongs

octagon

An octagon is a flat shape with 8 straight sides.

All these are octagons.

odd number

You cannot put odd numbers into groups of two.

1   3   5   7   9

odd numbers

old

Someone born a long time ago is old. Something is old when it is not new.

new

young

old

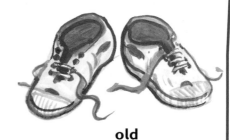
old

operation

Add, subtract, multiply, and divide are number operations.

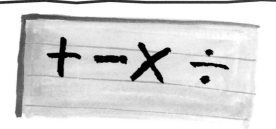

The signs tell you which operation to use.

order

Many things have an order. You write numbers and days of the week in an order.

order of days

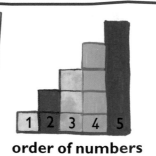
order of numbers

oval

An oval is like a squashed circle.

Some ovals look like eggs.

a b c d e f g h i j k l m n **o** p q r s t u v w x y z

a b c d e f g h i j k l m n o p q r s t u v w x y z

P p

is the **16th** letter of the alphabet.

pace

A pace is a step you take when you walk.

a pace

pair

A pair is two of anything.

a pair of socks

a pair of ducks

palm

A palm is the distance across your hand below the fingers.

A palm is the same width as 4 fingers.

part

You break things into parts. Parts can be equal or unequal.

4 equal parts   **4 unequal parts**

pattern

Some patterns have a part that repeats.

a striped pattern   **a spotted pattern**

pay

When you pay for something you give money for it.

She pays for her ice cream.

pentagon

A pentagon is a flat shape with 5 straight sides.

pentagons

a b c d e f g h i j k l m n o **p** q r s t u v w x y z

pictogram

A pictogram is a graph that uses pictures.

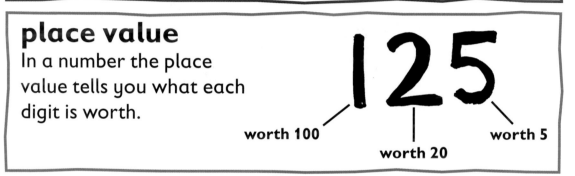

favourite fruits

orange   banana   strawberry   apple

place value

In a number the place value tells you what each digit is worth.

125

worth 100   worth 20   worth 5

plus

The plus sign is **+**. It tells you to add.

$2 + 4 = 6$

point

The points on a shape are the corners.

a point

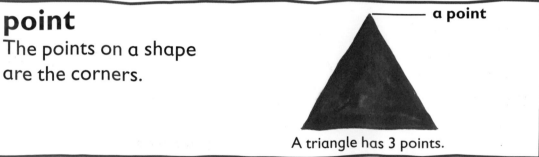

A triangle has 3 points.

polygon

A polygon is any flat shape with straight sides.

All these are polygons.

position

A position word tells you where something is.

up

left

right

in front of

behind

down

price

The price is the money you have to pay to buy something.

The price of chips is 75p.

pyramid

A pyramid has triangular faces that meet at a point.

pyramids

a b c d e f g h i j k l m n o **p** q r s t u v w x y z

Qq

is the **17th** letter of the alphabet.

quarter

When you divide something into quarters there are 4 equal parts. You can write a quarter like this $\frac{1}{4}$.

quarters

not quarters

$\frac{1}{4}$ one quarter

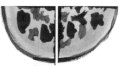

$\frac{2}{4}$ two quarters

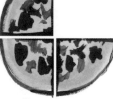

$\frac{3}{4}$ three quarters

$\frac{4}{4}$ four quarters

quarter turn

A quarter turn is when you make a quarter of a whole turn.

start

a quarter turn

a half turn

quick

Quick describes how fast something moves.

quick

quicker

quickest

Rr
is the **18th** letter of the alphabet.

rectangle

A rectangle has 4 straight sides. They join together at 4 right angles.

All these are rectangles.

reflection

A reflection is what you see when you look in a mirror.

mirror

reflection

reflective symmetry

Reflective symmetry is when one half is the reflection of the other half.

This flower has reflective symmetry.

regular shape

All the sides and the angles of a regular shape are the same size.

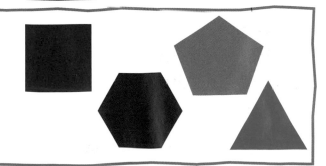

All these are regular shapes.

remainder

A remainder is what is left after you share something out fairly.

11 shared between 3 leaves a remainder of 2.

repeat

When something repeats it happens again.

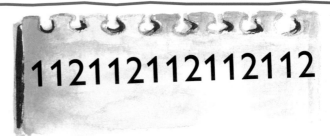

112 repeats in this pattern of numbers.

represent

Represent means "stand for". The pictures in a pictogram represent numbers or things.

Each picture represents one animal.

dog   cat   rabbit goldfish

right

One side of your body is the right side.

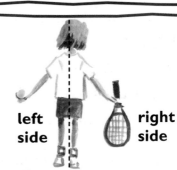

right side   left side   left side   right side

right angle

A right angle is a quarter of a whole turn.

a whole turn

a quarter turn

a right angle

rotate

When you rotate something you turn it.

round

A round shape has curves in it.

round sides　　　round edges

row

A row goes across from side to side.

Which are the even numbers in this row?

| 1 | 2 | 3 | 4 |
| 5 | 6 | 7 | 8 | — a row
| 9 | 10 | 11 | 12 |

The answer is 6 and 8.

rule

A rule tells you what to do to change a number.

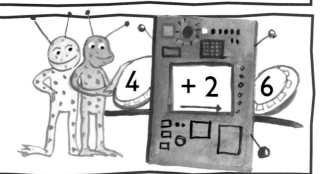

4　+ 2　6

The rule for this machine is add 2.

ruler

You use a ruler to measure and to draw straight lines.

a b c d e f g h i j k l m n o p q **r** s t u v w x y z

Ss is the **19th** letter of the alphabet.

scales

Some scales weigh in grams and some weigh in kilograms.

scales

second

A second is a very short time. There are 60 seconds in 1 minute.

Some watches have a second hand.

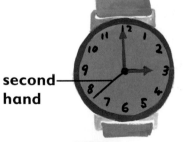

second hand

sell

When you sell something you receive money for it.

The clown sells balloons.

sequence

A sequence is a line of numbers. You make the numbers by following a rule.

3 6 9 12 15 →

The rule for this sequence is add 3.

set

A set is a group of things.

a set of red cars

shallow

When something is shallow it is not very deep.

shallow   **deep**

shape

A shape can be flat or solid.

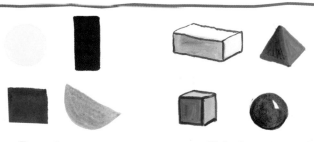

flat shapes   **solid shapes**

47

a b c d e f g h i j k l m n o p q r **s** t u v w x y z

share

When you share you divide things equally.

6 shared equally   **6 shared unequally**

short

You use short to describe the length of something.

short

shorter

shortest

The yellow caterpillar is the shortest.

sign

A sign is a short way of saying something.

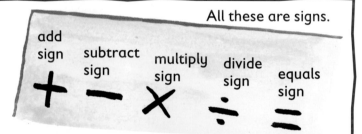

All these are signs.

add sign   subtract sign   multiply sign   divide sign   equals sign
+   −   ×   ÷   =

size

You measure something to find out its size.

slow

You use the word slow when talking about speed and about time.

slow   slower   slowest

small

You use small when describing the size of things.

small   **smaller**   **smallest**

solid shape

A solid shape has thickness.

All these are solid shapes.

span

A span is the distance from your little finger to your thumb.

You stretch out your fingers to make a span.

spend

You spend money when you buy something.

You spend money to buy shopping.

sphere

A sphere is perfectly round, like a ball.

All these are spheres.

a b c d e f g h i j k l m n o p q r **s** t u v w x y z

49

a b c d e f g h i j k l m n o p q r **s** t u v w x y z

square

The four sides of a square are the same size. All the corners are right angles.

All these are squares.

standard unit

You use standard units when you measure things.

kilogram centimetre
millilitre metre
litre gram

All these are standard units.

star

A star can have different numbers of points.

Here are some stars.

step

A step is the distance between your feet when you walk normally.

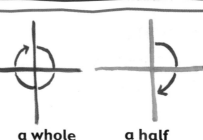

a step

straight angle

A straight angle is half a whole turn. It is the same as two right angles.

a whole turn **a half turn** **a straight angle**

50

stride

A stride is the distance between your feet when you take a large step.

subtract

When you subtract you take away.

You make numbers smaller when you subtract.

$6 - 2 = 4$

subtraction

Subtraction is taking things away. The sign for subtraction is — .

This is a subtraction.

$7 - 4 = 3$

sum

The sum is the answer you get when you add numbers together.

What is the sum of these numbers?

2, 3, 5

The answer is 10.

symmetrical

One half of a symmetrical shape is a reflection of the other half.

This ladybird is symmetrical.

a b c d e f g h i j k l m n o p q r **s** t u v w x y z

Tt

is the **20th** letter of the alphabet.

take away

When you take away you take one number away from another.

6 take away 4 leaves 2.

tall

You use tall when you talk about the height of things.

tall   taller   tallest

tally

A tally is a small mark to show how often something happens.

The tallies show that 3 people ate rolls.

tally chart

A tally chart has tallies for different things.

a tally chart

tape measure

A tape measure can bend and let you measure round things.

A tape measure can be quite long.

teen number

A teen number is any number from 13 to 19.

13 14 15 16
17 18 19

These are the teen numbers.

ten number

A ten number always ends in 0.

10 20 30 40

All these are ten numbers.

third

When you divide something into thirds it has 3 equal parts. You can write a third as $\frac{1}{3}$.

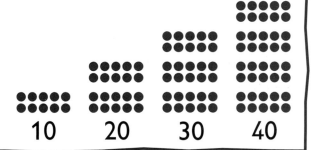

$\frac{1}{3}$ one third

$\frac{2}{3}$ two thirds

$\frac{3}{3}$ three thirds

times

Times is another word for multiply.
The times sign is **X**.

4 times 2 is 8
$4 \times 2 = 8$

a b c d e f g h i j k l m n o p q r s **t** u v w x y z

times table

You use your times tables when you multiply.

1 x 2 = 2	6 x 2 = 12
2 x 2 = 4	7 x 2 = 14
3 x 2 = 6	8 x 2 = 16
4 x 2 = 8	9 x 2 = 18
5 x 2 = 10	10 x 2 = 20

total

You find out the total when you add.

2   3   5

What is the total of these numbers?

The total is 10.

triangle

A triangle is a flat shape with 3 straight sides.

All these are triangles.

twice

Twice means two times.

Twice 3 is 6.

Uu

is the **21st** letter of the alphabet.

unit

You measure things in units.

These are measuring units.

1 metre   **1** kilogram   **1** litre

Units is also another name for ones.

There are 5 units in the number 125.

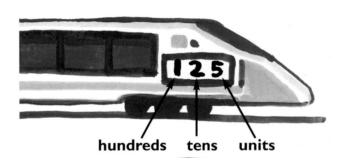

hundreds   **tens**   **units**

Vv

is the **22nd** letter of the alphabet.

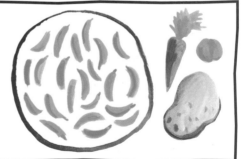

Venn diagram

You use a Venn diagram to sort things into groups.

This Venn diagram sorts shapes.

triangles   **not triangles**

a b c d e f g h i j k l m n o p q r s t u **v w** x y z

vertex
A vertex is the point of a shape.

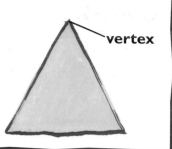

vertex

vertex

vote
When you vote you choose.

Three children vote for the colour red.

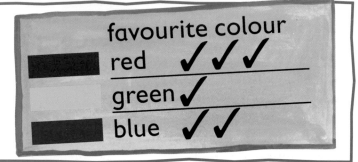

favourite colour
red ✓✓✓
green ✓
blue ✓✓

Ww

is the **23rd** letter of the alphabet.

week
A week has 7 days.

the days of the week

Monday
Tuesday
Wednesday
Thursday
Friday
Saturday
Sunday

weekend
The weekend days are Saturday and Sunday.

weigh

You weigh something to find out how heavy it is.

You can weigh yourself.

weight

You measure weight or mass in grams and kilograms.

You use a balance to find out the weight of a parcel.

You can use weights to find out how heavy things are.

whole

A whole shape is not broken into parts.

whole   halves   quarters

whole number

A whole number is not a fraction.

2 is a whole number

$\frac{1}{2}$ is a fraction

$1\frac{1}{2}$ is a whole number and a fraction

a b c d e f g h i j k l m n o p q r s t u v **w** x y z

whole turn

A whole turn is
a complete turn.
It is the same as
4 right angles.

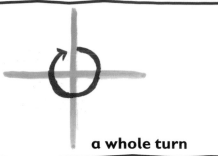

a whole turn

wide

When something
is wide its sides
are far apart.

wide   wider   widest

width

Width is the distance
across something.

the width of a river

Xx

is the **24th**
letter of the
alphabet.

X

You will see the letter X
written on some clock
faces. It means 10.

Some clocks have letters
instead of numbers.

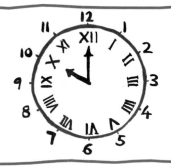

Y y

is the **25th** letter of the alphabet.

young

Someone born a short time ago is young.

young   **younger**   **youngest**

Z z

is the **26th** letter of the alphabet.

zero

Zero is another word for nothing or nought.

zero, nothing, or nought

a b c d e f g h i j k l m n o p q r s t u v w x **y z**

Numbers

0 zero	0 zero	0 zero
1 one	10 ten	1000 one thousand
2 two	20 twenty	2000 two thousand
3 three	30 thirty	3000 three thousand
4 four	40 forty	4000 four thousand
5 five	50 fifty	5000 five thousand
6 six	60 sixty	6000 six thousand
7 seven	70 seventy	7000 seven thousand
8 eight	80 eighty	8000 eight thousand
9 nine	90 ninety	9000 nine thousand
10 ten	100 hundred	
11 eleven	200 two hundred	1st first
12 twelve	300 three hundred	2nd second
13 thirteen	400 four hundred	3rd third
14 fourteen	500 five hundred	4th fourth
15 fifteen	600 six hundred	5th fifth
16 sixteen	700 seven hundred	6th sixth
17 seventeen	800 eight hundred	7th seventh
18 eighteen	900 nine hundred	8th eighth
19 nineteen		9th ninth
20 twenty		10th tenth

1st first   2nd second   3rd third   4th fourth   5th fifth

Days of the week

Monday
Tuesday
Wednesday
Thursday
Friday
Saturday }
Sunday } the weekend

Months of the year

January   31 days
February   28 days
(29 days in a leap year)
March   31 days
April   30 days
May   31 days
June   30 days
July   31 days
August   31 days
September   30 days
October   31 days
November   30 days
December   31 days

Time words

morning   afternoon   evening   day   night

Maths apparatus

abacus
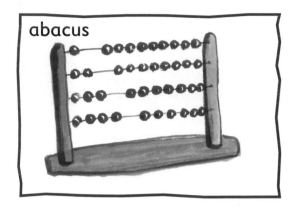

digit cards

balance
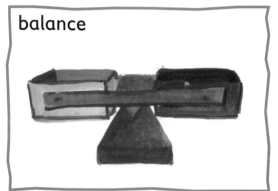

dominoes

calculator
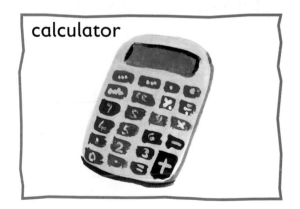

equalizer
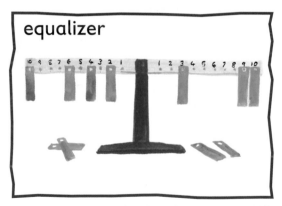

dice

geoboard

interlocking cubes

number rods

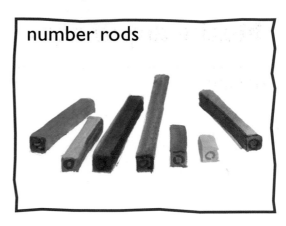

measuring jug

peg board

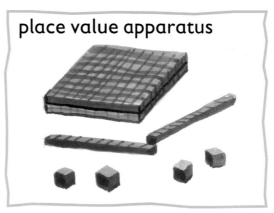

number cards

place value apparatus

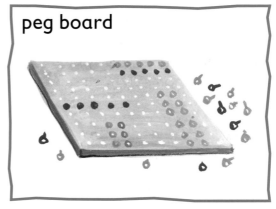

number fan

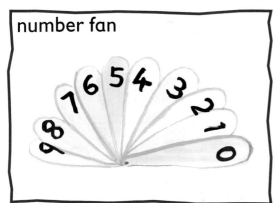

timer

Maths doing words

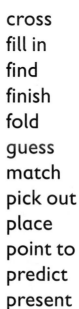

arrange	cross	record
build	fill in	ring
carry on	find	roll
check	finish	round to
choose	fold	shade
collect	guess	slide
colour	match	split
compare	pick out	tick
complete	place	trace
continue	point to	turn
copy	predict	use
count	present	work out